Becoming A Respected Leader

Becoming A Respected Leader

Growing Your EQ With Your IQ

Gregory Seymour

ARPress
ILLUMINATING IDEAS
EMPOWERING VOICES

ARPress
45 Dan Road Suite 5
Canton MA 02021
Hotline: 1(888) 821-0229
Fax: 1(508) 545-7580

Ordering Information:
Quantity sales. Special discounts are available on quantity purchases by corporations, associations, and others. For details, contact the publisher at the address above.

Printed in the United States of America.

ISBN-13:	Softcover	979-8-89330-740-5
	Hardcover	979-8-89330-742-9
	eBook	979-8-89330-741-2

Library of Congress Control Number: 2024902848

Dedication

I wish to thank all those that were behind me in writing this book.

A special thanks to the late Bob Johnson, who mentored me as a first-time manager. A man that understood emotional intelligence long before the term was created.

I also wish to thank the ladies in my life that were so supportive and encouraging. Thank you, and love you, Leticia and Jennifer.

Contents

Introduction i

What is Emotional Intelligence? iii

Terminologies 2

EI in your work life. 4

Leadership vs. Management 7

What Emotional Intelligence Is NOT . . . 11

The Yin and Yang of EI Management . . . 16

What is a respected leader? 20

The Challenges of Emotional Awareness . 25

Giving Emotions a Name 32

What is your EQ? 35

Growing your EQ 42

Utilizing your Emotional Intelligence in Leadership 54

Teen EQ 62

Steps to expanding your adult EI. 71

Non-Profit Leadership. 77

The balls in your court 84

References 86

Introduction

What you are about to read is a methodology that explains emotional intelligence. The goal is to demonstrate how to improve your EQ (Emotional Quotient/Emotional Intelligence) in a way that can help you to become a respected leader. It is easy to think that you're a great leader, but the real proof is in what others think of your leadership skills. Getting your people to accomplish goals is essential, but what is more important is what they and you endure to get there.

The most common excuse I hear from a hard leader is "That is the way my boss was, and I am just fine, as is evidenced by my becoming a leader." If you must cajole your people into reaching goals, odds are you are working under constant duress, and quite probably so are they. The big question is; Do they fear you or respect you? Differing fields require different management styles. The difference is that the leader that is EQ enabled and uses it wisely will become respected by their subordinates and peers. Why is this important? People want to work for a person they admire, and will, when necessary, go the extra mile for such a leader without hesitation or remorse.

Too many good employees leave their job because of poor leadership. Be the type of leader you would want leading you. Take the time to apply what you learn in this book, and if you focus on and utilize your EQ, you will see a change in your people within a year.

Understand that everyone grows at different rates, but by applying the concepts in this book every day will create a noticeable difference before you know it. I recommend that at the end of each day, you take a few minutes to review your day and how you dealt with the challenges of the day. Where do you think you applied your emotional intelligence, and where could you have better utilized this improving skill? As with most, one can go off track when first trying to implement a new method of communication, but refer back to the basics of this book, and start again. My goal is to give you improved skills that will not only make your life easier but will impact the lives around you at work, home, and socially.

Coming from a Psychology background, I understand when people say, "I don't have time for this at work." However, you will find that many challenges become harder from a lack of Emotional Intelligence skills, and you certainly don't have time for that!

What is Emotional Intelligence?

Emotional Intelligence (EI or EQ) is a term created by two researchers – Peter Salavoy and John Mayer – and popularized by Dan Goleman in his 1996 book of the same name. EI is the ability to: Recognize, understand, and manage our own emotions. Recognize, understand, and influence the feelings of others.

The first question to ask would be whether Emotional Intelligence Exist. To establish EI's existence, Peter Salovey, David Caruso, and John Mayor developed some concepts to measure EI. The team wanted to see if emotional intelligence abilities were measurable. Do such capabilities improved with age (knowing that intelligence generally improves with age), and does EI form cohesive knowledge. The team believed that if all those conditions were present, EI arguably would be an intelligence (Mayer John D).

An example of a test question they developed was to ask test-takers to identify the emotions they believed were expressed in a facial photograph. Another question asked people how reactions to emotions may have unfolded. Their sample question was:

George was sad, and an hour later, he felt guilty. What happened, in-between? (Choose one):

A. George accompanied a neighbor to a medical appointment to help out the neighbor.

B. George lacked the energy to call his mother and missed calling her on her birthday.

Test-takers achieving higher test scores determined that alternative B, (the missed birthday phone call) was the more likely reason for George's mood shift from sadness to guilt.

The concepts that encompass emotional intelligence (EI) are certainly not new. Classified as soft skills; they are crucial components to personal and professional success. The increasing interest surrounding emotional intelligence has raised questions about what Emotional Intelligence entails. The methods employed to measure it, how one can acquire or increase it, and to what extent it benefits an individual. Emotional intelligence encompasses self-regulation, self-awareness, motivation, empathy, and social skills.

Emotional intelligence means having an ability to not only identify your own emotions but to manage your feelings and to an extent, the feelings of others. According to Mayer, John D., there are three aspects:

1. Emotional awareness, which encompasses the ability to identify your emotions as well as those of others;

2. The ability to control your emotions and impart them to tasks like thinking clearly and abatingchallenges;

3. The skill to keep your emotions in check, as well as the ability to temper another person's emotions.

Being dominated by your feelings can be changed by acquiring stronger emotional intelligence skills. You can keep your emotions from getting in the way of a choice you will not regret later. Make your emotions work in your favor. Not developing these skills can put you more often in a victim position

Terminologies

EI- Emotional Intelligence, defined in the next chapter.

IQ- Intelligence quotient, measurement of intellectual level

EQ- Emotional intelligence quotient, is the measurement of emotional intelligence

Empathy - Empathy is a mental skill that enables a person not only to relate, but experience the thoughts, experiences, and emotions of people around them. Empathy is much more than the primary form of sympathy, which encompasses the ability to understand and support others with sensitivity and compassion. For leadership, empathy is a powerful tool of well-liked and respected leaders.

Compassion- this is an understanding of one's pain combined with the desire to mitigate said pain.

What is the difference between empathy and compassion? At times compassion is a broad reference to sympathetic understanding. Empathy is more of a vicarious relationship to another's pain, having prior similar experience. There are times when compassion is both a feeling and one's actions stemming from said feeling while empathy is often applied just to a feeling.

EI in your work life

Why do I need EI at work? Workers possessing high EQ will generally interact better in work teams, are easily able to adjust to change and be flexible. Contrary to the level of degrees or the acquiring of on-paper qualifications a person may possess, if the said individual doesn't have specific emotional qualities, they are less likely to succeed. As today's workplace continues to evolve, invoking newer technologies and innovations, emotional intelligence qualities become increasingly important.

Let's look at a couple of examples of emotional intelligence in play.

I am sure many of you have been in a meeting where everyone in the room starts talking over each other, and no one is actively listening. A clear sign that egos are at play and a lack of respect exist for coworkers. A clear demonstration of a lack of emotional intelligence in the room. When people are allowed to speak, without interruptions, and the others are actively listening, it's a clear sign that EQ is at play. It demonstrates mutual respect for coworkers and will most often lead to a constructive meeting.

Unlike pure and simple perceptions, our world is created by our emotions. Because emotions represent our values, when one's values become distorted, so does one's emotions. We then do things that are against our better interest or long-term interest. (Burton, PG)

Your level of Emotional Intelligence often changes over time, and when you make a conscious effort, it will become stronger. After testing yourself and defining what areas of weakness are present, make a simple plan to begin improving your EI. It is through daily efforts that you will bring awareness to the emotional reactions you have to different situations. A simple way to enhance your focus on your emotions is to utilize your smartphone. When you have an interaction with someone that you felt could have gone better, take time after the encounter to use the voice recorder on your phone and layout what transpired. At the end of your day, take 10 or 15 min to review your recordings and then think about what you could have done differently. For some people, doing this early morning before starting your day works better. The better option is to take a moment after the encounter (when feasible) to consider what you could have done differently.

High EI people, for example, can accurately perceive emotions in faces. Such individuals also know how to use emotional episodes in their lives to promote specific types of thinking. They know, for example, that sadness helps analytical thought, and so they may prefer to analyze things when they are in a sad mood (given a choice). High EI people also understand the meanings their emotions convey. They know those angry people can be difficult, that happiness means that someone wants to join with others and that some sad people may prefer to be alone. High EI people also know how to manage their own and others' emotions. They understand that when happy, a person will be more likely to accept an invitation to a social gathering than when sad or afraid.

The ability to answer such questions correctly seems to improve as children grow up. Also, such questions cohere as a group: People who do well at some items tend to do well on others as well. EI is now understood to exist and is considered by many to be an established intelligence.

Leadership vs. Management

"**C**ircles of influence vs. Circles of power. Just as managers have subordinates, and leaders have followers, managers create circles of power while leaders create circles of influence" (Nayar, 2013). The difference between managing work and leading people is that Managers control their people to accomplish a task or goal. Leaders, on the other hand, enable others, as well as motivate and influence their people, thereby becoming a part of the organization's success. In general, leaders inspire and influence, while Mangers utilize power and control. (Nayar, 2013).

In most cases, managers count value much more than they add it. Therefore, it is so important to be a leader in addition to managing. You need to not only calculate value but create it.

Management in retail is often misleading, especially when managing a corporate store. Let me give you an example of a corporate store releasing all controls to a store manager. My daughter worked for a major store and was being groomed to take over a substantial high-end store. She soon learned that the current manager had changed plans and decided to stay on as manager for several more years. She spoke with the area manager and asked about other opportunities within the company. They recognized that she had some strong skills, so they decided to send her to a store that was not making a profit and told her to take on the store and see what she could do. They chose to back off on controlling all aspects of the store, like most corporate stores, are regulated. They told her to do what she thought was best to turn the store around. Within ten months she managed to turn the store around and broke four corporate records for management during the short time she ran the store. She ended up opening her retail establishment shortly after. Because of her success, years later, she was picked up by another corporate retail store. They did not give her free reign but did loosen some restrictions, and she made the store become a healthy profit maker. They then sent her to a major anchor store to see if she could turn it around. This corporation also said they would let her have full control. The store started turning around, and slowly, management began stepping in and making decisions for her. The store began to struggle again, and she left. Ten months later, they asked her to come back and help with a new store with the caveat that she would be in control. It wasn't long before that they once again started making decisions for her, and the store struggled. She left again, very disappointed in them not sticking to their agreement.

Both corporations did not learn from their experiences with her. Why was she succeeding where other stores were not? The simple answer is Leadership instead of Management. She was aware of her emotions, her employees' feelings, and her customers' emotions. She focused on the needs of her customers in her area, as opposed to generalized corporate views of customer needs. Cookie Cutter Corporate Management and control in retail are partially to blame for the downfall of box stores.

The most significant difference between leaders and managers is that old-school management training doesn't teach one to speak their truth and find their voice. The last difference between managers and leaders is that being a manager in the old-school view doesn't require a manager to find their voice and speak their truth (Ryan, 2016). Most of the Corporate Management Training Seminars I attended back in the day focused on Time management, rules, and procedures. There was nothing about how to approach your boss with an outside the box idea or concept. During one of my reviews when I was in middle management, my boss complained. He said, "I tell you what to do, you say yes, yes, and then you go back to your office and do what you want." For the first time, I stood up to him to defend my actions. I explained to him that I could answer his concern with a metaphor.

I said when you paint with a roller, do you do so by rolling up and down? He said yes. I replied that I paint with a roller going side to side. Even though our methods are different, the result is the same. When the paint is dry, you cannot tell what direction, it was rolled on. The same thing holds true for how I do things at work; I do not think the same as you, and therefore will not do things the same way you will. However, the result is that I give you a completed project that you requested, in the time frame you asked for, with the results you were looking to attain. My methods don't take any longer than yours, but I achieve the same results, so please let me be me. He thought about it for a moment and said he had never considered this before, but he had to agree that I am giving him what he wants when he wants it. Management training of the time did not teach me how to do this; it was a faith-based step that I could convince him that my methods were acceptable. I demonstrated that not only was I a qualified manager, but a thinking leader.

A simple way of establishing whether you're a leader or manager is to take stock of how many people outside of your range of authority seek advice from you in the work environment. The higher the number that does, the more likely it is that people see you as being a leader. The competitive advantage is when you can be both a leader and a manager. You have great skill in leading your team, while at the same time being a manager of the day to day operation under your responsibility. Being agile, adaptive, and change-savvy is Leadership.

What Emotional Intelligence Is NOT

Both psychologists and journalists have falsely labeled Emotional intelligence to be something other than what it really is. Emotional Intelligence is not being agreeable, motivating, an optimistic view, happiness, or having a sense of calm. There is no question that these are essential qualities to have, yet they have nothing to do with actual emotional intelligence. There is an excellent article by Justin Bariso that you should consider reading (See reference list). His focus in the article is on what emotional intelligence is not. I agree with many of his points. Even though Emotional Intelligence or Emotional Quotient has only been around less than 40 years, the concept is quite old. Having a clear understanding of yours and other's emotions affords you the ability to make more informed decisions. Knowing how your coworkers will react to certain situations allows you to make decisions and choices that will garner more positive reactions and responses. It does not translate to not knowing how to avoid awkward moments but having the ability to identify when a challenge is coming and how you will react. Thereby reducing the possibility of having regrets later about how you dealt with the problem.

Another point that Bariso makes is that emotional intelligence does not mean it is a positive thing. Emotional intelligence can be just as thorough when getting people to do things that are not in their best interest. A great example is President Trump. While most would say he has no emotional intelligence, that is a false statement. He may not be empathic, but he understands how to key in on other's emotions and use them to his advantage. Most often true for many politicians.

EQ is used to quantify one's emotional intelligence level; it has its limits just like "IQ" does. Those knowledgeable in the field of emotional intelligence see the abbreviation as a symbol of a person's knowledge of theirs and other's emotions more than an actual measurement.

Let's look at all the EQ testing that is out there. While these tests can, in some cases, give an accurate measurement of one's emotional intelligence, it has its limits. As an example, while I consider myself to be reasonably intelligent, and have the knowledge and skills to build a house, I do not know how to, nor do I have the skills to build a rocket ship. The same holds true with emotions. Lifestyle and cultural background can dictate to an extent how a person's feelings will be impacted. So, while I may register as having a healthy emotional intelligence level, I would be less likely to register the same if I were working in a culture or environment, I know little about. Your level of emotional intelligence is limited (for most of us) to the social, economic environment in which you work and live.

Let's take a few minutes to talk about the nay-sayers on emotional intelligence. "One of the principal tenets of emotional-intelligence proponents is that awareness leads to behavioral change. They suggest that by reading a book, taking a test or going to a seminar you become more aware of your emotions and that, with practice, you will become a better leader and more successful at work" (Tobak, 2014). While he makes some valid points here, he is generalizing. Yes, some believe that awareness leads to behavioral change, and that is far from always true. The younger you are, the more truthful that is. However, for us older adults, we are not likely to see a great deal of behavioral change in our lives. Having said that, awareness is still a valuable tool.

I will use myself as an example of the importance of awareness. I suffer from a social disorder. Put me in a room of people I don't know, and there is a good chance I will depart having made no new connections.

I was an emcee at a cancer walk held at a high school. Near the end of the event, most of the people gathered in the bleachers with many still on the field, and I had no hesitation picking up a microphone and speaking to almost 900 people while standing on the track in front of them. It is the personal interaction that I struggle with until I am comfortable with the person. I dropped out of college after one year in 1971 and went back to college a few years back and finished with a Master of Science in Psychology. I wanted to have a better understanding of people and myself. My improved awareness has enabled me to be mindful of my social shyness and find ways to get past it at the moment.

Emotional intelligence is certainly not a method of curing all the world's problems. There is a darker side to emotional intelligence. It is essential to understand that emotional intelligence is "morally neutral." What this means is that while it is most often used to protect, help an promote others and oneself, it can also be employed as a tool to promote oneself at the cost of other people. At the extreme, emotional intelligence can be complete Machiavellianism, which is a method to manipulate other people to achieve one's personal goals socially. We all understand that success in life requires socially succeeding, which requires having keen emotional intelligence. Succeeding in life depends in large part on achieving socially, and a large part of the social success depends on EQ. However, as research has demonstrated, emotional intelligence can be utilized for win-win or win-lose outcomes. (Cummins, 2014).

People like President Trump are a clear example of this. Suppressing emotions and not being disagreeable is also not a part of emotional intelligence. It is more about cultivating emotional actions that work for you and not against you.

Understanding emotional intelligence via this writing is meant to give you a better understanding of what it is and the positives and negatives of such knowledge. Just because you are not able to improve your emotional intelligence doesn't mean you can't understand what it is and how to look for it in others, including those that you might want to work for, hire, or be associated. It is also imperative to understand when someone is using emotional intelligence as a weapon against you like President Trump has been able to do. Understanding it can protect you from falling into their misguided beliefs.

While we know that some have counterarguments to emotional intelligence in the work environment, the bottom line is that emotional intelligence is not an absolute requirement to succeed in business. Those that succeed without it are few and far between. There is no doubt that in today's work environment having a healthy level of emotional intelligence is very important.

The Yin and Yang of EI Management

The key to proper management is a balance. We often find that our leaders are either very forceful or very enabling. Generally, if they are more vigorous in their actions, then they will usually be less enabling. The same holds true for many leaders that are very enabling in that they are often not forceful at all. Employees often complain that when a leader is too heavy on one side, they exhibit very little on the other side.

The concept of yin and yang is to be harmonious. Being forceful when necessary and enabling when necessary leads more quickly to accomplishing goals. It is not just about having a vast skill set but having a skill set that can adapt to the constant changes and effectively reach set goals. It is ok to be forceful when necessary, but it should not be the default mode when things become challenging. It is this versatility that leads one to the level of a respected leader.

Because we are emotional creatures, things can sometimes get a little messy. In the work environment, we want to keep that mess to a minimum. While there are several areas where this applies, let's start with the two sides as they relate to emotions. There is the Less emotion preferred method and the Caring too much about your employee's approach.

Let's first look at the "less emotion preferred" method. Most managers feel that a touchy-feely approach to management is a big negative. They believe that one should not focus on an employee's feelings. They often see this as a sign of weakness from a management perspective and a distraction that they don't have time for. They think that emotions can override ethical decision-making. These managers will often steer clear of emotions coming up in the workplace in the hope that the employee or employees will figure it out on their own. These managers do not feel a need to coddle their emotional employees. Most often, they don't want to deal with the challenge because they don't know how to handle it. The problem comes in when employees see a manager as harsh, non-collaborative, uncaring, and even authoritarian jerks. In these circumstances, employees often are not performing at their best and have a "no skin in the game" attitude.

The absence of emotional intelligence on the part of management often impedes their level of effectiveness. It is also a possible sign of the organizations' cultural structure that experiences constant turnover in people. It is these types of organizations that expect the best from people without considering such a fundamental personality trait. This type of management thinks that focusing on people negatively impacts performance levels. To have a cohesive team of workers, a focus on performance and emotions must co-exist within the organization.

On the other side of the spectrum, there is the "I care too much about my employees" method. The downside here is that when giving out assignments, the overly touchy-feely manager tries to make sure there are no hard feelings amongst the employees about their task assignments. Often this leads to a lack of focus on performance levels, as well as making some employees feel like you are trying to be their therapist. They then feel like the manager is over-involved in their life. It can distract the employee from meeting performance goals (Sporleder, 2010).

A balance of yin and yang feeds innovation. Innovation is not just about the product, but about the inside of the organization. Most important is better internal and external communications, along with improved incentive systems. It correlates to happier employees.

What does this mean for you as a leader? Projecting an image as a balanced leader is one part, but it is also imperative that you are an internally balanced leader. It is this inner balance that has a direct correlation to your actions and choices.

It is this balance in you that is critical to creating motivated employees having faith in your leadership. Then they experience a more pleasurable work environment. It is at this point that they will be willing to go above and beyond to accomplish the goals of their department or team. Additionally, it will also give the reward of having long term employees that work towards the vision of the organization. Your employees will also feel more empowered.

A great quote by Jim Rohn is "The challenge of leadership is to be strong, but not rude; be kind, but not weak; be bold, but not bully; be thoughtful, but not lazy; be humble, but not timid; be proud, but not arrogant; have humor but without folly."

What is a respected leader?

The Oxford Dictionary defines respect as "a feeling of deep admiration for someone or something elicited by their abilities, qualities, or achievements."

For those that do not respect their leaders, they are merely saying they don't have any admiration for your achievements, abilities, or qualities. When this happens in the workplace, production generally falters.

Garnering respect most often creates a healthy work environment. Your employees perform at a higher production level, and work challenges become much more comfortable to resolve. What qualities must a manager have to gain the respect of their subordinates and peers? Words are powerful. Speak well of your coworkers and employees. Never fail to give credit to those that deserve it. Harsh words don't help when an employee is having challenges. Encouragement and guidance do.

Employees do better when there is a meaningful reward system in place. When you are in error, admit it and remedy the situation as quickly as possible.

You are demonstrating that you are human like them and can not only acknowledge your mistake but take the right steps to remedy the situation. Don't make promises you can't keep. Trust in you is critical to success. Create clear communication paths and show your people that you are accessible and open-minded. Make hard decisions when needed. Demonstrate that you have boundaries and will not let a break in those boundaries affect other employees. Never be afraid to ask for input or advice from your team. Demonstrate a willingness to be open. Rules and regulations are not all that make a company successful; it is also about your people and how you treat them. Know your business and take responsibility for your actions. Be a good listener. It is one of the essential points of being successful as a leader. Let your people know that you see the big picture and delegate work appropriately. Have faith in your people's abilities. You hired them because they had the skills needed for the position. Micromanaging can all too often create hatred and confusion. Give respect and show interest in an employee's development. Lying to your people is the fastest way to lose any respect you may have earned. Being humble beyond your ego goes a long way.

When you help make your employees look good, you automatically make yourself look good in the eyes of others. Confidence instills confidence in your people. When a problem arises, focus on solutions, not anger and blame. Solve the problem, then communicate clearly on future prevention. Set a standard with your strong work ethic. Help promising employees to grow. All these things combined are the foundation to becoming a truly respected leader as opposed to a demeaning and spiteful leader.

Avoid over-estimating yourself. It is vital that you learn and grow in your position and help your subordinates do the same. Taking the approach that when voicing an opinion, you would like to hear other's views, then discuss the differences and potential reasoning behind them. You will earn respect if your leading by example.

Evolve and encourage others to do the same as your business evolves. If people do not respect you, they will not give their all for you. Be open and engaging. If you demonstrate that you care about who they are and what they do, they will gain respect for you. Never demand respect, earn it by your actions.

Another critical point is when making a mistake, own up to it, resolve it quickly, and learn from it. When things go very well, be sure to share the accomplishment. Please don't take all the credit but give credit where it is due. Always try to be as transparent as possible. Some secrets are essential, but that should be the exception to the rule.

A great quote from Theodore Roosevelt is "The best leader is the one who has sense enough to pick good men to do what he wants done, and self-restraint enough to keep from meddling with them while they do it."

Leaders that are concerned about the careers of those that work for them will rarely have to worry about their job.

One more significant area necessary to becoming a respected leader that is often a tough one for leaders is humility. For myself, years of low self-esteem has worked in my favor when becoming a leader. I do my best always to be humble. I have difficulty at times with accepting praise. I find it more soothing to deflect any praise to my team. I believe that if I focus on my people and make them not only look good but be good, then I will be successful. When someone does make a mistake, I don't let anger be the first reaction. The first thing I focus on is resolving the problem, and then when time permits, I discuss the issue with the person making a mistake. Sometimes I will discuss it with the whole team, pointing out what led to the error and the steps that can be taken to prevent it from happening again. Most often, I find that focusing on a solution first (while everyone else is focused more on the person making a mistake) is best. I can help that person to settle down more quickly and take away any guilt that might be on their mind at the moment.

Another critical step is to share authority when possible. I have overseen a video team at my spiritual center for many years now. While I very much enjoy being the director during a service, I select team members to step in and learn to be directors as well. I guide them initially, then let them learn on the job. We discuss any challenges they may have faced later. When appropriate, I tell them that we have all made said mistake before, and it is a learning experience. As a volunteer team, and they enjoy coming each Sunday to dedicate their time. Having been shown by me that they are of great value, and they get to learn new and exciting aspects of the operation. On the few occasions that I am absent, they have attained the confidence and skills to step up and get the job done.

Because I receive a fair amount of positive praise as their leader, I always remind myself that it is not all about me. It is important to graciously accept their compliments because not doing so is signaling to them that they are wrong in doing so. I receive the praise and then put it aside and remind myself to be humble. I am not the fantastic leader they say I am. I'm a good leader that they all too often don't get to experience in their other work environments. Doing the right thing does not make one amazing by comparison. It just makes me different from what they usually encounter.

A key element to becoming a respected leader is the ability to balance being fair and caring, while at the same time remaining firm on your convictions.

The Challenges of Emotional Awareness

Your emotions play a vital role in your daily life. Not only for you but for the people you have relationships with, be it personal or work-related. Your emotional reactions to everyday activities can telegraph your mental state at the moment. You can come across as flippant, angry, overly excited, happy, sad, or depressed. Too much excitement over a simple thing can project a sense of immaturity. Improper responses to a tragic story can project a sense of rudeness. Unexpected anger can present you as being unbalanced. As adults, we are expected to restrict our emotional reactions and feelings (Whitbourne, 2012).

Simply put, the ability to recognize emotions you are having at any given time is emotional awareness. To be able to manage those emotions, you must first be able to identify what your feeling. Emotional awareness has different levels. It is Drs. Schwartz and Lane's theory that there are six levels of increasing emotional awareness.

It starts with having no emotional awareness. It is where you have no idea if emotion is present, or you are unable to sense any feelings. An example of this could be "I feel like I am a real loser." Saying you feel this way is, however, is not an emotional state, but just a simple self-judgment. Adding the word feels too I'm a loser doesn't make it an actual emotional feeling. Having said that, you can feel physical sensations. Then there is level two, bodily sensation awareness. You may feel your muscle tension or that your heart is racing, but it is not an emotional feeling. You can also feel pain or discomfort, but again, this is a bodily sensation.

Level three is the awareness of your behavior. At this level, you may only be mindful of an action you would like to take as a result of a situation. As an example, it could be that you want to get away from a situation, but you don't know why. The actual emotion could be anxiousness or fear-based, but you don't recognize that.

At level four, you may be mindful of an emotional state being present, but you can't establish what that emotion is. You know you are feeling something, but that is as far as it goes. You may think that you are presently overwhelmed, but you can't describe what the actual feeling is. This level has an undifferentiated emotional state. There are times when undifferentiated emotions lead to dangerous situations. At this level, a person can resort to yelling and screaming and even, in some cases, physical aggression. Usually, this happens when a person is unable to find the right words to express the many emotions that came up just before expressing anger. This level of ineffective communication often leads to strained relationships and often limits one's degree of happiness.

Level five is where most people are, in general. Most people can distinguish what their genuine emotions are, and this establishes them as being healthy-minded. At this level, one is clear on what specific feeling is present, and often why they are feeling this emotion.

This final level, level six, is referred to as blended emotional awareness. It is considered the top level of one's emotional awareness. Not only are you aware of your emotions at this level, but you are mindful of multiple emotions present at one time. An example of this could be that your daughter is getting married and moving away. You can be both happy that she is getting married and sad that she will be moving away.

It is from Drs. Schwartz and Lane's theory that the (LEAS) Levels of Emotional Awareness Scale was developed and is still today utilized to evaluate and research emotional awareness.

Most people understand that our outward display of emotions impacts other's opinions about the type of person you are. Culturally, this can vary. The types and levels of your feelings are perceived differently in various cultures. Having control of your emotions gives the impression that you are functioning within the cultural norms of your society. We now know that all cultures recognize fear, anger, surprise, disgust, sadness, and happiness. It is how they express these feelings that can vary by culture. Typically, our emotions impact us more than they do to those around us. An important point to understand is that our emotions are a learned response. It is not something we are born with and can't change.

Before we get farther into methods of controlling your emotions, let's delve in a little way to the psychological interpretations of emotions. The perspectives we have garnered over the last century have certainly changed with the early beliefs about emotions centered around a bodily response. An example would be running away from a bear in the woods. The James-Lange Theory and the Cannon-Bard theory did not stand up to scientific scrutiny. The Cannon-Bard Theory focused on the thalamus as controlling emotions. While it does have some involvement, the amygdala is where jealousy, fear, and rage begin.

It wasn't until the 1960s that Stanley Schachter and Jerome Singer developed a new theory. Their belief that emotions were controllable bore out a conclusive result that both context and arousal influenced one's emotional state. In other words, your feelings can be affected by the environment you are in at the time. Emotional contagion is the term for this.

Don't be misled by this, though, because your emotions do not have to be triggered by those around you. There was a cognitive revolution in emotion theory, led by the University of Pennsylvania psychiatrist Aaron Beck. Beck demonstrated that at the root of people's feelings of sadness, there were dysfunctional attitudes in depressed people where they formed negatively framed automatic thoughts. A dysfunctional approach consists of having a world view with a focus on unrealistic and negative aspects of one's experiences. Emphasizing your weaknesses over your strengths is an unconscious belief of negatively framed automatic thoughts. It is Beck's theory that has created the cognitive-behavioral method of therapy, which even today is considered the treatment of the premier depression.

Baring being clinically depressed, there is still much to learn from Beck's research. A belief that you will or have lost something vital to you can bring forth the emotion of sadness. Believing that someone has taken away something valuable to you can stir anger. Moreover, if you have this belief that something terrible is about to happen to you, you will develop anxiety. It is often the unrealistic distortion of these things that lead you to have strong negative emotions.

It is psychologist Albert Ellis that developed that cognitive theory concept of "musterbation." These are emotions controlled by a must. "I must be Successful," "I must be loved." "I must have what I want" Ellis created an ABC model of emotion.

A is the activating event, added to B, which is one's belief, and would equal C the Consequence (emotion). The challenge, of course, is that to change the outcome, you must change your thinking. To accomplish this, you must examine the basis for your belief. Once you can find the hollow portions of a view, you can find ways to change them. Once you accomplish this, you free yourself from being dominated by these false emotions (Whitbourne, 2012).

So, we have looked at the formulations of your thoughts, lets now look at your facial feedback. There is a facial feedback hypothesis that supports, "The idea that one's facial expressions can affect the emotional experience." An Example of this is "A woman attending a stuffy party forces herself to smile, and finds she feels happier as a result" (Grinnell, 2016). The activation of facial muscles can trigger mental changes that will mimic the corresponding mood. Sad expression, you will feel sad, happy feeling, you will feel satisfied. Thus, the thought process behind the phrase "put on a happy face." Employing facial expressions means your gut, or even the amygdala won't control you. Placing a focus on your thoughts just before your emotional reaction will assist you in managing your mood (Whitbourne, 2012).

Now that we have looked at the basic science behind emotions, what should you be doing to maintain a healthy emotional state? Start by monitoring your various levels of emotions and formulate a habit of doing this. You must first understand yourself before you can look at understanding others. Take a few moments throughout your day to think about what your emotions have been as your day progresses. Monitor these emotions and try to do a short recap of your day before going to bed.

Being able to increase your emotional awareness will take some time and dedication — definitely a skill

GREGORY SEYMOUR

worth refining. If there are times when you are not able to immediately identify your emotions, remember the scenario leading up to these emotions. It will help you to establish what was going on with your feelings at the moment.

As an example, if you are sensing that something terrible might happen and you notice that your heart rate is increasing, coupled with the fact that you understand anxiety and fear are typical emotions, you can rest assured that you are feeling fear and anxiety.

It is when you formulate a habit of emotion monitoring that you will progress up the ladder of emotional awareness. Understand also, that keen emotional awareness gives you a more solid foundation for learning about other people's emotions.

Giving Emotions a Name

hile many of us aren't aware of our emotions at the moment, they have a powerful impact on our work quality and focus. If we are not mindful of what the emotional impact will be while performing our jobs, we can more easily become frustrated, confused, or even angry. Instead of asking yourself or others how you/they are doing, ask how you are feeling right now. Unfortunately, most employers don't give emotions much thought. They prefer that you park your feelings at the door as you enter work. The simple truth is that as humans, our emotions are not parked at the entrance to our workplace. They may be hidden, but they are still there and having their impact on your day.

When you are performing at your peak, please take a few moments to think about your feelings now and come up with an adjective to describe it. Most people label these moments of peak performance as optimistic, confident, open, positive, calm, happy, focused, and enthusiastic. These are the times when we feel most productive and recognizing these feelings will help us to maintain our attitude longer, thereby remaining at a peak performance level.

Now when we are not at our peak, but feeling our worst, people, in general, will assign names to their feelings. These emotions consist of irritability, pessimism, negativity, defensiveness, self-doubt, impatience, and unhappiness. At this level of feelings, our vision can narrow, we consume more of our energy, and our sense of value may feel at risk.

Imagine that you sense a serious threat to your physical well-being lurking in the shadows. Then you're asked to solve a complex problem. How will you perform? In this "fight or flight" state, you would struggle to think clearly or imaginatively, and it would be difficult to collaborate effectively (Schwartz, 2015).

For most, we traverse the entire field of emotions throughout the day, with many expressed and some hidden. These emotions revolve around how we are experiencing our day.

An emotion that often hidden while in the workplace has to do with suffering. It is not a new thing; it started a long time ago. What is different now is the ever-penetrating demands placed on us, leading to uncertainty, anxiety, and feeling overwhelmed.

At this point, you may be asking yourself where the value in all of this is. The answer is that naming an emotion helps reduce its impact, which then lessens the mental burden. Dan Siegel, a psychologist, calls this practice "name it to tame it." Also. When we don't notice an emotion, we are unlikely to change (Schwartz, 2015).

It is also essential to understand that avoiding or hiding your feelings doesn't help them to go away. It also does not reduce their impact on our mental state.

Recognizing, and naming your emotions provides us with the opportunity to stop and think what your feeling and what is the best choice to make from here.

Emotions are an energy source within you that is continually seeking to be expressed. Naming and claiming our feelings allow us to take full responsibility for them and then adapt or change them to prevent them from unduly impacting those around us (Schwartz, 2015).

What is your EQ?

I can tell you that my first thought process relating emotional intelligence was in 1971 when I started working for a major insurance company (CNA) in Chicago. I was a 19-year-old that dropped out of college after one year. They hired me along with three other young men for training in the same job. Two of us were only high school educated, and two were college graduates. After being trained side by side for a year, I formed an opinion about the two college-educated coworkers. I saw them as being "book smart" where my other less educated coworker, and I seemed to be more "street smart." This observation relates to having or not having practical intelligence. EQ was formulated as the alternative "street smarts," while "book smarts" correlates with IQ. At four years into the job, my coworker without college became a supervisor over the rest of us. Two years later, I became an assistant manager of another unit within the same department. The two college grad coworkers never moved into management. I am not bragging or saying that college did not help others in their careers. It was just an observation at the time that there was a difference in our thought processes, unrelated to formal education. This difference, unbeknownst to me at the time, was our emotional quotient.

It is essential to recognize the possible benefits of EQ over the long haul. Studies to date have been scarce. Social Capitol building relates directly to EQ as a network of social support. It is those with a higher EQ that will seek out mentors to train or expose them to new ideas and concepts. Thus, enabling them to better qualify for the higher paying leadership positions.

Let's look at the advantages of having a high EQ. Most often, people with high EQ's have multi-level advantages. They can first identify, regulate, and comprehending their own emotions where it affords them the ability to better communicate effectively with others. Thus, they can face challenges, form healthy relationships while doing so, and often maintain the new connection for a more extended period. This emotional management becomes a valuable tool in a variety of ways, especially in the workplace environment. All too often, we must compete for limited resources within the company, and work through the office "politics." With a higher EQ, you can balance these strong relationships and better navigate through the political and social office environment. The more you understand the sometimes-complex makeup of your organization, the more effective you will become.

It is most often the person with a high EQ that will go out of their way to help others. You may be showing someone some more straightforward methods of accomplishing a task, or tips on dealing with specific situations. When your actions assist people, they will be very appreciative, and often come back to you more often for answers to questions they have. When you mentor others, others notice, and, in many cases, this can result in a pay increase. It can lead to the people you help forming stronger bonds with you and seeking out additional guidance from you. They will also see you in the light of being a senior person.

On the other side of the coin, leaders, or coworkers with low EQ levels all too often are seen as bothersome and painful to work alongside. Overbearing bosses, or coworkers that are overly intrusive into your personal life can make your experience a lot less pleasant. They often talk too long, consistently throw roadblocks in your way, and can be overbearing in meetings. These people are usually low on the popularity list, and struggle to find acceptance. They often feel left out and passed over without understanding what has led to that.

Understand that having a high EQ will not, in itself, make you wealthy, but it will help place you in a better position for advancement within the organization. Not only will you derive more emotional pleasure from your work experience, but you will often find it to be more financially rewarding.

Determining your EQ is not necessarily simple because it is too easy to get a false EQ evaluation level. The number one challenge to getting an accurate read is frank with yourself. Secondly, the EQ test that you take should focus on the area of your life that your focusing on for the test. In other words, your EQ for your work could be a bit different from the EQ result you get when focusing on your personal life. Therefore, some of the professionals that write about emotional intelligence don't have much faith in EQ testing. It is critical that you be honest enough about yourself. Then the test will be a reasonably accurate indication of your EQ for both your work and home/social life. There is also the issue that some tests are better indicators than others. I also highly recommend that you have your significant other, family member, friend, or coworker take the test as it relates to their view of you. Comparing results will help in finding areas where you may not have been honest with yourself about the test you took. Compare the results and rethink some of the answers where others disagree with what you have said. Keep in mind that they may not know as many things about you. It will help in giving you a more accurate idea of where your emotional intelligence level is. Then look at what areas may need more focus to improve your EQ.

Which EQ test should you take? These tests typically apply to organizations, individuals, and teams. Currently, there are three basic methods of testing.

First, is the self-report test, which relates to your ability to recognize emotions in others. Second, is the 360-degree feedback (like I said previously with other people's view of your level of EQ). Third, is for your performance and abilities. This third method is again, what others perceive your ability to recognize how other people emotionally react to situations.

Research suggests that the performance-based or ability test method produces a more accurate assessment of your EQ level. Your management team will be able to assess your strengths and areas of challenge to better assist you in making improvements in the work environment (Langley, 2012).

It is important to note that for self-reporting and 360 testing, there can be bias. The result of you not being candid in your examination and can also be a factor. The person testing on your behalf has some negative bias towards you, and therefore, is not being honest in the test process either. They can also be biased if they are trying to make things better for you when answering the questions. The level of accuracy relates directly to the level of honesty.

Emotional intelligence tests encompass a variety of measures and targets. Based on their ratio of capacity, they cover behavior, trait, competency, and ability.

The current research-backed EQ tests are:

1. Mayer-Salovey-Caruso Emotional Intelligence Test (MSCEIT)

2. EQ-i, EQ-i 2.0 and EQ360

3. ECI or ESCI

4. Genos EI

The focus of each test is that the MSCEIT test is abilities based (much like an IQ test). The Bar-on EQ-I analysis is trait-based focusing more on the social/emotional aspects. The ECI test is competency-based focusing on learned capabilities. The Genos EI test is behavioral-based focusing on one's demonstrated behaviors (Langley, 2012).

So, we have the abilities based, trait-based, competency-based, and behavioral-based methods of testing. Which one should you utilize and why?

The abilities-based test (MSCEIT), like the IQ test, focuses on abilities, but from an emotional aspect. It focuses on your cognitive skills to resolve emotional challenges. The creators designed this test through their concept of Emotional Intelligence. This test is most often used for recruitment and can cut through the false impression a job applicant my try to give of themselves.

The trait-based test (Bar-on EQ-i) relates to one's disposition or personality. Like the Meyers Briggs test, it looks at traits of introversion and extroversion. Seen as the most commonly used trait-based test as it relates to emotional intelligence. It was structured on the Bar-on model of EI utilizing an Emotional Quotient Inventory (EQ-i, EQ-i 2.0, and EQ360. There is also a TEIQue test that is like this test.

The competency-based test (ECI of ESCI) reveals one's emotional intelligence in comparison to what is considered normal levels in society. The higher the level of leadership, the higher the results are expected to be. ECI is the Emotional Competency Inventory, and

ESCI is the Emotional Social Competency Inventory. These two tests conform to the model developed by Dan Goldman and Richard Boyatzis.

The behavior-based test (Genos EI) measures the frequency of one's actions and behaviors. They based this test on the belief that these skills are teachable. The test was initially designed for the workplace in Australia.

While these tests have pros and cons, look at what your needs are concerning your organization. Choose the test that compliments each other and are not copies of each other. If your organization is not yet using these tools, I suggest that you research the organizations that are. Then inquire as to their reasons for choosing a particular test.

Growing your EQ

efore you can start raising your EQ, it is essential to understand what actions or thought processes people with high EQ don't do.

According to Travis Bradberry, there are nine things emotionally intelligent people don't do in general.

Start with not letting another person limit your joy. Other people can define your happiness if you fall into the trap of comparing yourself to them or listening to the opinions of others about one of your accomplishments. You are in control of your happiness. You are never as good as or bad as they say. It doesn't mean being emotionless; it means to absorb what the person said with a grain of salt. Remember, your self-worth will generate from within yourself.

Second is not forgetting. It means not holding a grudge, but being quick to forgive, without forgetting. If choosing to give a person another chance, be aware, and don't let yourself get strapped with other people's mistakes. Let go quickly, don't forget and protect yourself from possible further harm by them.

The third is not to "die in the fight." Don't keep fighting a battle that can leave you damaged. When emotions get out of hand, irreparable damage often occurs. Know the importance of living to fight another day. Stand your ground when it does more good than harm.

The fourth is not to prioritize perfection. Trying to be perfect is like chasing your tail. You will not get there. We all have our faults. When you expect perfection, you always end up being disappointed. It leads to a sense of failure. Be proud of what you have accomplished, and always look for ways to improve when possible. Enjoy what you have accomplished.

The fifth is not to live in the past. Placing focus on your failures eats away at your self-confidence. Often, failure comes from taking a risk and trying something new. Getting it always right the first time is not how things work. Almost anything you are trying to achieve will take a risk, and failure is not complete if you learn from it. Focusing on past mistakes does not help you move forward.

The Sixth (which is not dwelling on problems) ties in with the fifth. That which you place your attention on establishes your emotional state. If you dwell on the past issue, you will not find it easy to focus on a solution. You improve your efficacy when you focus on actions that better yourself as well as your circumstances. Focusing on a solution is much more effective.

Seventh is to not hang around negative people. Have you ever noticed that complainers are continually talking about their problems? They think that gaining others' sympathy will make things better. It is ok to take a little time to listen to them, but you can't let yourself get wrapped up in their negative downward spiral. Try to set limits where possible for being around this type of person and keep your distance when possible. One way to establish your limits is to ask the complainer what course of action they plan to take to resolve the problem they are facing.

The eighth is not to hold grudges. You are creating a stress response when you hold onto a grudge. Merely thinking about it puts you in a negative frame of mind. Researchers at Emory University have demonstrated that when a person holds onto stress, it often leads to high blood pressure and heart issues. Remember that holding onto a grudge is like you taking poison and expecting the other person to die.

The ninth is not to say yes unless you want to say it. The University of California in San Francisco conducted research that demonstrated the more difficulty you have in saying no to a person, the higher your stress levels will go. It can lead to depression and even burnout. When necessary, be firm in your response, and don't use phrases like "I don't think so" or "I'm uncertain if I can." Say no and state your reasons clearly (Bradberry, 2014).

I will bring up other things that people with a higher EQ don't do as we work on things to help you grow your emotional intelligence.

Let's start with some basics. Take time to begin studying your own emotions and how you react to various situations at work, at home, and socially. What are your reactions when someone gives you criticism (helpful and non-helpful)? How do you handle driving in heavy traffic? You come across someone who is visibly emotionally upset. What if your best friend or partner blames you for something. Look at all the things that impact your day, and how you react to them. By first getting an idea of where you are emotionally, you can better assess what changes would benefit you in the future.

Take an online test and ask a partner or friend to take it as well from how they see you. Remember, honesty is paramount here. Look at any variances between the two tests and discuss them with the other test taker. See if you can agree on where you are at this time. Honest answers will produce accurate results. If there were a question that the two of you do not agree on, I would suggest taking the other persons point of view if you trust them.

Now you have a baseline with which to work. Now you need to start focusing on your reactions to situations throughout the day. As I mentioned earlier, set aside time at the end of your day to review your actions for the day.

Place your focus on where you think you could have handled a situation better. Don't dwell on what you did wrong but focus on what you can do to be better. That which you focus on comes to fruition, so concentrating on the negative will only bring more negative. Your body is energy, both physically and mentally. Take that energy and direct it in a positive way to grow in the direction you want to go.

An example of this is from a decade ago. I was facing some severe health challenges and was no longer able to perform the work to keep my business going. After losing everything, I knew that I had to go in a different direction. It took some time and effort, but I decided to no longer focus on my pain and struggles. Instead, I looked at where I thought I wanted to go in my changed life and started placing all my attention on my new goal. I had a few short-term jobs in the interim to keep my self afloat, but I decided that I needed higher education. I had initially dropped out of college after one year back in 1971. I had always disliked school, so it was a difficult choice to go back. I chose to focus on just an associate degree so that if it didn't work out, I wouldn't waste too much time and money.

An essential step in moving forward and making changes is not to keep your focus on the goal all the time. It can seem very daunting this way and lead to discouragement. Instead, focus on each step toward your goal while keeping the target in the back of your mind. Each level is less daunting and often more manageable. After completing just two classes, I realized that I could accomplish much more and then set my sights on a bachelor's degree. I was so pleased and excited at getting my degree that I continued to attain a Master of Science in Psychology degree. If I had placed my focus totally on the Masters in the beginning, it would have seemed difficult to achieve since it would take me five years to get there. Under the circumstances, at the beginning of this journey, I would have taken a negative outlook that it was just too far away.

When coaching clients, we are continually setting short term goals and discussing how they are doing and what is interfering, if anything. The step I take when they are struggling with doing it in the time frame, they wanted is to encourage them. My example to them is; If from point A to point B is 15 steps, and you slowly keep taking each step, you will always reach point B.

The process I would like you to keep in mind as your work on growing your EQ. You may have an occasional setback and beat yourself up about it but keep moving. A parishioner once asked a wise minister a question. The person stated that they were going through hell at the time, and what should they do. His response was, "Don't stop there and build a condo, keep moving." Again, don't stay in the negative.

For each person, methods of improvement vary, so first learn what methods work best for you. Start with yourself and being more aware of your emotions every day. I highly recommend that you keep a journal of some type. Considering the vast array of electronic devices, you can even do an audio journal on your phone, or jot notes on your phone/tablet/computer. When possible, make these notes or audio files throughout the day. Again, make time at the end of each day to review your day and update the journaling process you are using. As you review your notes or recording, you will begin to see patterns of behavior. Place your focus on the responses that need improving.

An essential part of this self-awareness is looking at the root causes of your emotional reactions. Don't just recognize that you yelled at someone; look deeper into why you made that choice. What about that particular situation led you to your reaction? Do you have anger issues? Alternatively, is it more likely, like most of us, where we have days that seem to get progressively worse, and your patience wears thin?

When your day is heading in the wrong direction, you should be aware of and understand what is happening and take steps to adjust your emotions. You can take a break, take a short walk, or find a temporary distraction that will help you to settle back down. Also, take time to look at how you have been reacting to the earlier parts of your downward day.

Let's focus on some specific steps you can take to grow your EQ. Start by making a connection between your feelings and thoughts. When an uncomfortable feeling arises, take a moment to ask yourself when you felt like this before. Is your reaction based solely on what is happening right now, or is it based on how you felt this way before? You could have a mix of feelings at the moment. Take a little time to think through the emotions, look at the current situation, and make a sound decision on how you should best react to the situation. See the bigger picture here. When you have an emotional reaction, ask yourself if you have felt this emotion before, and how you reacted then, and whether it is appropriate to respond the same now or differently.

It would help if you also listened to what your body is telling you. Are you feeling butterflies before the first date? Maybe it is because you have higher expectations this time. Got a knot in your stomach about a work situation? Perhaps the stress means you're not prepared for what is about to take place. Allow your body to work with your emotional state.

It is also crucial not to stifle your feelings too quickly. Let your feelings happen and think them through. Our emotions most often peak and fade quite naturally. Please don't interrupt the feelings until they have at least hit their peak. Usually, when we are not feeling very comfortable in a situation, we will try to change the subject to distract from our current emotions. Take time later to think about what you were feeling and why.

There are times when we are unsure of what we are feeling. If possible, a trusted friend or coworker can tell you how you are coming across. Their insight can sometimes be an eye-opener.

As I mentioned earlier, write your feeling down, or record notes on your phone or tablet. It is a way of expressing your feelings while keeping them private.

You should also refer back to them on occasion and consider if you would act differently now, and why. It is also an excellent time to focus on your unconscious feelings. You can do this by putting yourself in a relaxed state of mind and allowing your thoughts free to roam about and pay attention to where they go. Also consider analyzing your dreams, again record this through written or voice recording. You will want to pay particular attention to the desires or thoughts that repeat themselves or are highly emotional.

One advantage to voice recording your feelings each day it that you can hear yourself talk. Pay attention to the emotions behind your words. It can also be an eye-opener.

I recommend that you take just a moment each morning to ask yourself how you are feeling to start your day, and then ask that same question at the end of your day. If it has changed notably, ask yourself why. You can even create a rating scale for each day.

An important point to keep in mind is that there are times when it is best not to be looking inward but looking outward. Understand when it is time to place your focus outward and be present in the moment you are in. Emotional intelligence encompasses both your inner and outer world.

Know what causes you stress. While we can't avoid stress, when possible, address stressful situations when you are best able to deal with them. Be mindful of your words. Your vocabulary is essential to have excellent communication skills. Often in meetings, many technical terms or acronyms are used. Be sure that the people you are communicating with can understand what you are saying. Keep in mind that the emotions behind our words can influence how people will react to them. Always be aware of your negative emotions. Being demeaning or condescending works against you. If a person is causing you to be upset, don't jump to conclusions. Think about it objectively and move forward from there.

One of the keys to emotional intelligence is empathy. Focus on the verbal and non-verbal cues given off by your coworkers or employees. Try to imagine yourself in their shoes for a moment. Sometimes when someone is acting poorly, a calming statement can help them. It will remind you that everyone has challenges and deals with them differently. This action does not excuse the unacceptable behavior but helps to diffuse the situation at the moment.

When adversity strikes, your response is what determines your level of success, or you can fall into a pit of despair. To bounce back from adversity, one must place their focus in a positive direction. Make your attention solutions-oriented, and the quick rebound from the problem will make you feel much better. Transform your self-deception into self-awareness.

These are the things that you can do to evolve the level of your emotional intelligence over time. It is when you begin to see results that your desire to continue to do so will grow. Then when you feel like you're making progress, become observant of others and how their emotions played into the various situations throughout your day.

As you grow your EQ, you will find it easier to help others build theirs. You attain career success when you pay due attention to your employees and coworkers. For people with lower EQ levels, it is quite challenging to see things from other people's perspectives. Often this results in closed-mindedness when there is no obvious right or wrong way to approach a project. When you take an other-centric approach, team success is more likely by having a better understanding of team members' strengths, weaknesses, and belief patterns. Open-minded team conversations lead to a solution that all members of the team can accept.

Research has demonstrated that people who are "rewarding" to deal with are more employable and enjoy a more successful career path. Rewarding people are those that demonstrate unselfishness, are more trusting, cooperative, and friendly. Unrewarding people tend to be more critical, pessimistic, and argumentative. While some may view this type of person as having high standards, it usually leads to relationship erosion and a reduction in productivity. It is not only important to proactively share resources and knowledge but to do so without the expectation of reciprocity.

In most work environments, you can find employees that have a naturally higher level of emotional intelligence. First, recognize them and what they are doing with their coworkers. Most often, people with higher EQ's will be the ones helping other employees by sharing their knowledge and skills with them. Giving recognition to these people in front of all employees will often encourage others to be more helpful. It will foster the growth of others' emotional intelligence. Encourage all employees to take coaching (not management) approaches to each other. Keep in mind that this will require people having a more open mind in their workplace. Be careful not to let personal biases creep into the environment. Talking down to others is not coaching; it is demeaning. Treat each other as equals in the process. The coaching may only entail one specific area of the work process. It need not be all-encompassing. Remember that we all have our strengths and weaknesses. Let other's strengths feed our shortcomings.

Many organizations/corporations are not as hierarchical today as they once were. They perform their work functions across teams, not just within them. They even work cross-departmentally. Encouraging this often leads to a more productive environment. Helping newer employees to work this way keeps the operation from slowing during the learning curve.

Utilizing your Emotional Intelligence in Leadership

Now that you have the basic concept of emotional intelligence, along with the pros and cons. Let's delve into its use in leadership.

In the work environment, there are challenges relating to technical aspects, supply and demand, and many other pieces. However, quite often, the challenges faced daily are from a human perspective. So, we need to first talk about cause and effect. Cause and effect are defined as having a relationship between events or actions in such a way that they are a result of the other or others. A simple example would be my cause of flipping a switch results in the effect of the light coming on.

Our emotions are directly tied in this fashion. Some cause or action has resulted in an emotional effect that one produces from such cause or action. Depending on the cause, the effect will be in the companies' or employees' best interest or it will not. The higher the EQ of the leader, the less likely these adverse outcomes will arise.

Let's dig deeper into utilizing emotional intelligence in leadership. We will start with five essential elements of emotional intelligence that support effective leadership.

A meaningful organizational identity needs to be established and maintained. Develop Collective objectives and goals.

For change and decision-making, flexibility needs to be encouraged.

It is essential to generate and maintain trust, optimism, confidence, cooperation, and enthusiasm. Appreciation of work activities needs to be instilled in others. A leader needs to possess the ability to develop work goals that employees can get excited about, along with excitement about specific job duties while instilling confidence and positive attitudes. Creating a "go with the flow" attitude encompassing flexibility while having an organizational identity that is meaningful to the members (Ackerman, 2019).

Current research suggests that there are six leadership styles.

Coercive/Commanding: This is seen as the harshest style because it involves immediate obedience and compliance. Typically using a phrase like "Do what I tell you."

Authoritative/Visionary: getting people to move towards a preset vision. Typically using a phrase like "come with me."

Affiliative: Spawns harmony growing emotional bonds. Phrased as "people come first." Democratic: Establishes a consensus of participation. Phrased as "What do you think." Coaching: Development of people's strengths for a better future. Phrased as "Try this."

Pacesetting: Establishment of higher standards relating to performance. Phrased as "Do as I do, now!" (Stevenson, 2014)

It is essential to understand that these styles are not exclusive, nor are they overall good or bad. Varying situations require the use of one or more of these styles, and a leader may find it necessary to adopt the different methods in a given case.

Determining what style is called for by a leader is an integral part of applying emotional intelligence. EI/EQ can apply in differing ways for each leadership style. The chart below breaks down the various components of emotional intelligence within each style.

Style	Underlying EI Competency
Coercive/Commanding	Achievement, drive, initiative, emotional self-control

Authoritative/ Visionary	Self-confidence, empathy, change catalyst, visionary leadership
Affiliative	Empathy, building bonds, conflict management

Style	Underlying EI Competency
Democratic	Teamwork, collaboration, communication
Coaching	Developing others, empathy, emotional self-awareness
Pacesetting	Conscientiousness, achievement, drive, initiative

When I first started a real job for a store while in high school, my experience with the manager was an eye-opener. He was brash and demeaning and never acknowledged when I would go the extra mile. In his eyes (as he would tell the young girls behind the lunch counter) he was a great boss that got things done! After many months of his attitude and treatment of others, I found another job and left. The point I am making here is that I was a good reliable worker that he lost because of his actions. Employment in the store was a revolving door. He never understood that his lack of emotional intelligence drove good employees away. He always had more work on his hands because he was constantly spending his time training new people. He even complained once about teaching people a job only to have them leave. He was frustrated with the effect but was unable to recognize the cause. He also complained that he didn't have time to deal with us. However, in actuality, if he had worked WITH his people, he would end up with a longer-term seasoned crew that would have given him more time to deal with other issues. The phrase penny wise and pound foolish comes to mind. He couldn't spend a few moments here and there to give a practical tip or compliment a job well done, so he spent many hours training new employees. I am sure many of you have had this experience as an employee more often than you care to remember.

I should point out that one of the reasons I focused on the managers I worked for was because I wanted to ascend to that level one day. My father had told me in my early teens a saying he learned and didn't know where it originated. He said, "Learn from others' mistakes because you don't have time to make them all yourself."

Another example of emotional intelligence in leadership at play is when I worked for a large corporation and became a supervisor over a unit with five employees. I took the time to have a one on one with each of them to give them a chance to know me, and I know them. One woman I talked with said that she had a complaint. She said that management doesn't understand their employees and their needs. I asked her to elaborate, and she did. I said I would do my best to make changes that would make her feel better. Less than a year later, she applied for and got a new job in another department as a supervisor. Approximately 4 or 5 months later, she came to my office to talk to me. She complained that her people don't understand the responsibilities she has as a supervisor and that she was not getting along well with some of them. I reminded her of the first time we spoke when I became her supervisor. I said that she complained that management didn't understand the employee challenges, and now she was saying that employees don't understand management challenges. I told her that she had forgotten from where she came. Treat your people the way you expected treatment when you were the employee. We discussed some of the changes I made back when I was her new supervisor and how things had gotten better for her.

For her, let's look at the cause and effect. What came out in our discussion was the statement she made about not trusting her people. We discussed the fact that she did not know her people. She didn't meet with them individually when she became their supervisor to get to know them and them to know her. I asked her what her basis was for not trusting them since they were already doing the job before she arrived. She had no answer. The big question was whether her trust issues were about them or herself. She is new in the position, never having supervised before, so what was her confidence level. The cause was her uneasiness with herself. It created the effect of anxiety on her employees. Focusing on the core problem will lead to a longer-lasting solution.

Several months later, I visited her in her office and asked how things were going. She said that things were improving, but she recognized areas where she still needed work. She said that after the first time she came to me as a new supervisor, she didn't think that what I told her was going to work. Because she was too busy, but she tried a few things and couldn't argue with the results months later.

When first promoted to a management position at the age of 26, I was quite nervous. I knew I was hired for a good reason but hadn't yet had an opportunity to see what I could accomplish. I was so very fortunate to have a Vice President that I reported to that was very people oriented. He said in our first one on one meeting that he saw potential in me as a people person and he was going to show me how to improve on that. I had the honor and privilege to be mentored by him for almost two years. When he retired, I was amazed at how many people from other areas of the company came to bid him farewell and state that they would miss him. I now recognize that he was so well-liked because he had a very high EQ. He was unique for his time (late 1970's). His focus was on people and how best to interact with them. He was a firm leader that also emphasized compassion and empathy. He understood his people very well and knew what it took to motivate each person individually.

When I began to apply the concepts that he taught me, it was a little challenging at first. I soon realized that this was not an overnight project. It took time and effort to get to understand each person working for me. Another challenge was to get to know the people under the supervisors that reported to me. I found that I had to be careful not to upset a supervisor by dealing directly with their subordinates. I soon learned that casual conversation often garnered more understanding of an individual that was not direct reporting to me. The discussions would include simple references to their jobs that would help me to understand their motivations and needs better. I also found talking to the supervisor about each of their people helped me to not only understand their employees better but to understand the supervisor's views on each of them better. It led to me being able to coach the supervisors reporting to me as I learned more about how they were dealing with their people.

Teen EQ

crucial area when it comes to the future of our society. It is during the teen years that one can learn the most about shaping their behavior patterns. Enabling them to acquire social intelligence through a better understanding of their own emotions and how to control them. It is today's teens that will make up the workforce of the near future. It is so important for teens to learn how to be reflective, empathic, and adaptive.

The is no question that today's teens face a great deal of stress. Teen stress has always been an issue, but with today's social media, it has grown significantly. Teens are lacking necessary skills for dealing with stress having a higher incidence of disengaging in both the classroom and among their peers. Having a higher level of emotional intelligence affords teens the ability to deal with stress and mood swings more effectively.

Teachers, instructors, and most importantly, parents need to improve their level of emotional intelligence so that they can recognize challenges in teens with whom they are interacting. Most importantly, a parent that understands emotional intelligence is better equipped to help their young teens. Guiding them in developing the skills that will allow them to deal with the constant pressures and changes they are experiencing in their growth is critical. Thereby leading them to a path to independent thinking and actions. There are questions that parents and teachers can ask at a minimum of once per week.

Keep in mind that your teen may be hesitant to answer such questions. I recommend that you use an approach or wording that you know would work best with your teen.

Questions like, can you tell me something interesting that you learned today? In your group project, what challenges do you face?

If there has been conflict within the group, how have you dealt with it?

Were you distracted in class today? If yes, what do you think was bothering you to cause the distraction? How are you feeling when it comes to taking exams or tests?

Do you have any challenges when trying to study? What can you do to make tomorrow a better day?

Have you helped a friend or classmate recently, and if so, what did you do?

What were the best and worst parts of your day, and how did you deal with them? Is there something you are grateful for this week?

Necessary actions you can take as a parent relates to understanding that they will face a barrage of positive and negative emotions. Be a guide for them by explaining appropriate ways to express negative feelings.

Help them understand that everyone reacts differently to situations, and they can learn from you and others by observing reactions that are acceptable and unacceptable. Explain the difference between emotions and behavior. Most emotions are acceptable, but not all actions are acceptable. Demonstrate ways for them to deal with negative emotions. Please take a few moments to settle down and think through your feelings or journal what they are feeling and then read through it later. Show them proper ways to express their emotions.

Guide them in coming up with solutions to challenges and learn to trust your child to find the best solution at the time.

Observe your teen with their peers to see how they are forming positive relations with them.

Discuss the topic of empathy. When you understand why you react the way you do to situations, you will begin to understand better why other people behave in a certain way. While we can't control other people's behaviors, seeing things from their perspective will help you to better empathize with them.

Try using a current example to explain this. Let's say that your teen had a classmate that was mean to them. Explain that the mean reaction by the classmate may be caused by them having a bad day. Suggest that instead of getting mad at the classmate, have your teen ask the classmate if maybe there is something, they could do to help them. It will demonstrate to their teen classmate that they care about them and have compassion for what they are going through. It also helps to end conflicts effectively.

Teens that can self-asses and recognize when they are becoming upset or frustrated will be able to act on those feelings healthily.

There are more and more programs being made available for teens to learn how to improve their emotional intelligence. Try to take an active role in their getting into and working through the programs. Whenever possible, attend programs together.

One of the best ways to teach your young teens about emotional intelligence is to model it at home. Demonstrating how to react to situations acceptably can be the best teaching method. When you can show how to de-escalate a situation, they will see the benefits of modeling such behavior.

As a parent or an essential adult in a teen's life, you represent to them the very best the world can be. If they sense that you are often critical and judgmental, they will likely mirror that in their lives (Young, 2015).

Take ownership of who you are. Acknowledge your imperfections, and they will learn to acknowledge theirs. Allow them to get things wrong and fail on occasion. We all have our off days and demonstrate that same ability in yourself. It is all a part of living and relating to others in society. When you make a mistake, let your teens see that you own said mistake. They will then be more likely to come and talk to you about their mistakes. The other benefit here is that you will strengthen their connection with you.

Listening to today's world seems to be more challenging than in the past. We have so many distractions and electronic gadgets that steal our time. Teaching this skill will be much more challenging for your teen as you will need to have them put down and shut off their electronic devices to accomplish this. When they say something to you, repeat it back to them to show that you are listening and ensuring that you understand them correctly as well.

After listening, it is vital to be able to negotiate differing views effectively. Allow them to disagree with you sometimes without trying to force them to change their minds. Let them know that you understand what they are saying but based on your experience or knowledge, you see it differently. Know that understanding them is not an agreement but is a demonstration of respect for their point of view or opinion.

For the most part, don't hide your feeling from them when it is appropriate as it can cause them to feel off-balance or 'less than.' We all run the gamut of emotions in life. We all get insecure, scared, jealous, mad, and sad. When you do share your feelings, be sure not to pour your troubles onto them.

Maintaining a healthy connection to your teens is the best way to have a viable influence on them. When they come to you with a big problem, it can be a shock. Try to remain calm, take a few deep breaths, and demonstrate behavior that will encourage them to be honest, show them how much their willingness to talk. Discuss clearly what action they need to focus on changing and why. Their relationship with you creates a foundation for their association with others in society.

There is an essential reason for one's feelings showing up:

Anxiety – ups our energy level to deal with a potential threat. If the anxiety relates to one's performance, reframing it as excitement can work in your favor.

Fear – peaks our energy level to deal with a dangerous fight or flight situation.

Anger- results from something being wrong and raises our energy level to put things right.

Jealousy- this is a complex emotion that can encompass fear, anger, and anxiety. It can often be painful as well but helps us understand the importance of behaviors that maintain essential relationships.

Sadness- most often, this feeling makes us step back from the outside world and reset, recharge and heal, and projects to others that we might need some loving.

Addressing the feeling will provide clues about what's needed to find more balance in our lives. It is a good idea to suggest that your teens find the words or some images that reflect the feeling. What is important here is for your teen to be recognizing their self-awareness and their capacity to observe those feelings. Thereby making them more aware of what they need.

Let's look at some essential points about emotions. Our emotions come and go as we often experience varying emotions throughout our day. Some feelings last only moments and others hang on leading to a mood. Emotions can run the gamut from mild to wild or somewhere in between. While emotions themselves are not good or bad, what is good or bad is how we express those emotions. Understanding how to express feelings or manage emotions is a skill in and of itself.

Bad feelings relating to friendships tell us that those friendships aren't the best ones to be in and that it may be time to let that friendship go. A fundamental piece of social and emotional intelligence is the ability to read and respond to relationships. Their decision about whom they allow close is always theirs to make. Try to encourage your teen, sans judgment, to think about their friendships in terms of how those relationships make them feel. What are they getting emotionally from the relationship? How would they feel without it? Does it bring out their best or the worst side? These can be challenging things to think about and to answer. However, the sooner they can develop this mindset and own their power to choose whom they let close, the happier they'll be.

When a relationship is terrible, they will know because it feels awful. Should a relationship do damage, it is evidence of a personal deficiency on either or both sides. Your teen needs to know that this is rarely true. People are driven to mistreat others by their inner history and hurts. Your teen mustn't become a target for someone else's dysfunction or pain.

Let them keep the friendship if they choose. Fighting with your teen on this often leads to their holding tighter onto the poor relationship. Let them know that they have the ultimate decision on staying friends.

Teens need to build confidence to relate to others, but there is a fine line between building trust and over-inflating them. Give praise as often as possible when earned. Recognition is like currency, and your teen should have the capacity to earn plenty. When praising them, do so for how respectful, hardworking, active, funny, kind, or brave they are.

At the heart of a thriving relationship is empathy. It is the ability to comprehend what others are experiencing and feeling. The simplest way for your teens to learn this is by observing you. As a parent, notice what they're feeling, identify it, and show them you understand. 'Let them know that you are observing them seeming mad, confused, or sad.' Doing this, will help them experience firsthand how empathy makes a difference (Young, 2015).

As a teen, and as an adult, emotional awareness leads us to know and accept who we are. To develop this emotional awareness, we can start with a few simple steps.

Start by making a habit of observing your emotions as they come forward and what situation triggered the feeling. Maybe you notice feeling stressed or nervous before taking a test. Perhaps you're excited about making plans to do something with a friend. Listening to music can bring up emotions of feeling upbeat or maybe feeling very relaxed. Observe the feeling and give it a name in your head. Notice how emotions can fade quickly or not. Next, you can rate the strength of your emotion on a 1-10 scale with ten being the more intense level. When possible, share your feelings with someone close to you or someone you trust. It helps you to put your emotions into words. It can include something rather personal or just an everyday emotion. As in sports and music, the secret to learning this is practice, practice, practice.

As you develop these skills, take time to observe others around you and how they react to a given situation and to what level their emotions rise and fall.

Steps to expanding your adult EI

We have established that Emotional intelligence is not intellect but encompasses an individual skillset. There are people with high IQ's that possess no emotional skills, and people of average or less intellect. So, what steps will help you develop your emotional awareness?

A more straightforward way of improving your emotional intelligence is to recognize your stress sources and be consciously aware of them as they come up. You can generally relieve these stress inducers through a calm approach like deep breathing, yoga, or meditation. For some people, the venting method works better like going for a jog, privately letting out a scream, or using a punching bag. Figuring out what stress reducers work for you will move you towards a higher emotional intelligence level.

I remember a time when I worked for a major corporation and an assistant vice president in my division had a bottom weighted blow-up clown about 4 feet tall in her office. When returning from a stressful staff meeting that didn't go her way, she would tell her secretary to hold her calls for ten minutes while she vented. She would close her office door and proceed to kick and punch the clown around her office. She would then come out of her office and be very calm and non-confrontational toward her staff. It seemed both strange and funny to me at the time, but it worked for her. She was never seen taking her frustrations out on others.

Another action you can take is to Name your emotions. Emotions can feel like a mighty wave that is pushing us along, and we are on an uncontrolled ride. Neuroscience research has developed simple steps that help us calm these pushing waves. Research has shown that naming our emotions can lessen the strength of emotions, by merely focusing our cognitive light on what we're feeling. Another method is to name your emotions in the third person. The point is to distance ourselves from our experience. Now for many, like myself, saying Greg (your name here) is frustrated feels too odd. So, instead, I would say, "Frustration is a present feeling in me." What this does sub-consciously, is distance the emotion from being you, thereby becoming a calming action. It does not mean you should forget or deny the emotion, because emotions are a form of information for us to deal with (Freedman, 2018).

Be aware and name an emotion when it comes up and experience it for a few moments. Society tells us that some feelings are bad, but they most often are natural. Don't just push the feeling away because it usually comes back later in an even bigger form.

Experience it within, understand what it is causing it, and then take a breath and move forward to deal with the situation that brought up the emotion.

Studies have shown that chemicals in the body are released from an emotion. It takes an average of six seconds for the body to then dissipate said chemicals within your body, so give yourself time to let that process take place.

It is also imperative to recognize recurring emotional patterns. When said emotional stimulus comes up, my reaction is to.

Doing this is an integral part of transforming your emotional outburst. Psychology and neuroscience taught us that thought processes travel through existing neural pathways. Therefore, we have recurring patterns of reactions or emotions. The good news is that one can change these recurring patterns through focus and re-adjustment of our emotions.

Emotions are a data source that helps you to see things more clearly. It is when we stop ignoring them, fighting them, or feeling like the emotion is suffocating us that we create a resource for change. Understand why you are having the emotion and move towards a better course of action (Freedman, 2018).

While emotional intelligence recognition is slow to grow in the major corporations around the world, it is certainly not a trend. Several major companies have compiled statistical data on the subject. It reflects how employees that have and employ emotional intelligence skills have a positive impact on the company's bottom line. These companies are seeing higher levels of productivity and total sales.

Developed emotional intelligence skills are fast becoming a vital part of one's professional success.

A vital place to start is with your listening skills. Psychological studies have shown that an emotionally intelligent individual engaged in conversation will listen intently to the other person to gain clarity. People often are listening to the other person peripherally until their turn to speak. Additionally, emotionally intelligent people observe the nonverbal details of the conversation. It will lead to fewer misunderstandings and allows the emotionally intelligent listener to project a level of respect to the person with whom they are conversing. A good listener must also be open-minded, or they will tend to shut down listening to the other person rendering the conversation unfruitful.

Understand the power of your attitude. A negative attitude is more easily infectious to coworkers. When you understand the moods of others, you are more likely to guard your approach to ensure an acceptable reaction. When faced with attitude defeating situations, take a deep breath, and then take a little time to meditate or have positive emotional sayings on your desk or walls. Maintaining proper health also impacts one's attitude.

When experiencing an instance of conflict, anger, and emotional outburst are common. It is the emotionally intelligent person that is more likely to stay calm and think things through before making a decision. One must remember that in conflicting times, you need to stay focused on the goal of resolution. Your actions and words at this time are critical to aligning with a resolution.

As a leader in these types of situations, a positive yet levelheaded response can garner one more respect without appearing either too passive or aggressive. Communicate your needs and or opinions respectfully. Setting high standards for yourself sets an excellent example for your employees. Show initiative and demonstrate strong problem-solving abilities.

Most people having keen emotional intelligence tend to be very good in leadership roles. They will tend to have rather high standards for themselves and are proficient in setting good examples for others. Having strong problem-solving skills, decision-making skills, and taking the initiative is often the norm for these people. It is what often leads to higher production levels and performance levels of their people. Utilizing an excellent yet assertive communication style and responding instead of over-reacting to conflicts affords these leaders decisive resolutions. A significant requirement in resolution skills is active listening. This type of leader will always strive to keep a positive attitude through the ongoing practice of self-awareness. These leaders "get it" that empathy is an emotional strength trait and not a sign of weakness. They will relate better to others and show mutual respect and understanding when opinions differ.

A big part of accomplishing this is their ability to handle criticism with dignity. Look at where the criticism is originating and how it impacts others. Also, see how it affects you so that you can constructively resolve the issue. They also can pick up on the emotions of others and how those emotions will impact a situation. Understanding this affords them the ability to read body language and how best to use the information to have clear communications with others.

A key component of having high emotional intelligence is that one is seen as more approachable, thereby opening the door to more ideas and information.

Non-Profit Leadership

I want to take a little time to discuss Leadership roles in Non-profit organizations. I am going to slip into my leadership coaching role for this chapter. Those of you that are involved in non-profit organizations are probably aware that there is a plethora of advice given to them. In general, people in non-profit leadership roles are expected to be a "Jack of all trades" type of leader. When you step into this type of leadership role, you want to be innovative, caring, supportive, supported, and open-minded. You want to utilize your most persuasive skills first to build a support team. In the early stages of your leadership, it is not uncommon to face several "Type A" personalities that will want to push for their agendas. It is where emotional intelligence will help you to deal decisively with these challenges. Strength, empathy, active listening, and clear communication skills are essential here. Keep an open dialogue and acquiesce when appropriate. As a leader, it is crucial not to let your ego get in the way of what is vital for the organization.

A personal example of this is when I became President of the Board for a Non-Profit Organization. The outgoing president wanted to remain in control of the board proceedings. When I first tried to make some necessary changes, I was not only confronted by her, but by her closest fellow board members. They wanted to remove me from the board. Fortunately, one new board member spoke up and said that they all should at least listen to what I am proposing. I knew that I had to do something drastic to retain my position.

So, what I did was to set up a meeting with the former board president several days before the next board meeting. We had lunch and discussed the current goals and benefits the organization provided for the community. I slipped into my coaching role with her by asking questions instead of saying I had an idea. As an example, instead of saying we should do X, I asked her if she has ever thought of X, and what was her input. She provided her input, and I asked a few more questions until she agreed with what my original intentions were. I then said, "I like what you're thinking, why don't you bring it up at the board meeting."

What transpired at the meeting was that her close supporters agreed with her. We then happily voted for the change. I had these meetings with her each month for several months when things finally turned around. She became a business friend, and she would say that she and I discussed an idea and that she thought my idea was good for the organization.

What I had to do in the beginning was to let my ego go and make her feel she was in the lead for a while. Once I could demonstrate to her that my ideas were worth discussing. Within six months, the rest of the board looked at me as being a strong leader for the organization.

The point I am trying to make here is this. If you are walking down a path in the woods, and you come to thick, dense brush in the way, do you hack and fight your way through it, or do you backtrack a little and find an alternate path that will then lead you back to the original route.

If you have a previous board president or chair that is a good leader, seek out their mentorship. Most will be more than willing to give you tips and guidance that will not just lead to successful leadership, but a successful organization.

For many new board leaders, the feeling that you may be lacking in some skills is normal. Quite often, after leading for a while, they find that they got appointed to the leadership position for the skills they already possessed. Be aware that micromanaging can be your worst enemy. Have faith in those you are working with or make changes to get people that can stand on their own two feet.

As a leader, if you feel you are weak in a skill set, look to another member that is strong in the skill set and tap them to take on the task. Then work with them to improve the skillset for yourself. An active board is generally strong because of the diverse skills of its members. When you capitalize on your strengths and create a team that capitalizes on their strengths and skillsets, you will all tend to move the organization forward in a positive way.

When you step into the leadership position, take a deep breath, review your strengths and weaknesses. Please get to know the skill sets of the other people on the board and employ their skills wisely. Take time to look at what you want to accomplish as a leader. Understand that you should only have two or three main goals as a leader. Having a laundry list of items often leads to disappointment for yourself. Meet individually with each board member to become better acquainted with their skill sets and their reasons for being on the board. You know that being a board chair is a passion project, not a job. It holds true for the other members of the board as well as the general membership of the organization. Learn the day to day operations of the organization, and you will have a better idea of where the organization needs growth or change. Ask questions of the daily operations staff and be mindful of their knowledge. Active listening is required here also. While you will not always have all the answers, you need to understand where to get the solutions. That more often will come from within the organization but can come from outside as well. Learn to ask the right questions.

Often when asking questions, especially of staff, you will get the classic, because that's the way we have always done it. Times are ever-changing, so asking the right questions could lead to better methods of doing things. Keep in mind that some methods are already the best method in place.

When actively listening to other board members or staff, keep an open mind. If the answer to a suggestion is no, it is imperative that you give a good reason why that is so. Not doing this will cause people to think you are not open to new ideas because you always say no. If they understand why you are saying no, they will rethink their concept. If they believe it is viable, they will present a better idea. Creative thinking is a vital part of non-profit organizations. Don't stifle it. Additionally, sharing knowledge is indispensable for the organization.

Concerning your goals for the organization, it is essential to be aware of the impact your changes will have on others, especially if there is staff. They may have to do more or need more help to accomplish the growth or changes. While it is likely that you have worked with the organization for some time, you may know all the areas needing attention. However, it is unlikely that you can manifest changes to all of them during your term. Again, keep to two or three goals for your term that you have determined are the most important currently and that have the backing of your board members. Prioritize your goals and stay focused. Keep in mind that sometimes, challenges come up that may become more important than your first priorities. Sequence them and know that addressing the new issues are as important, if not more, than your initial goals. Being flexible is essential in the non-profit world.

Also, be aware of the capacity of the organization. Lofty goals may not be in the best interest of the organization. Goals are generally not accomplished overnight, be focused, but have the patience to see the way through.

Staying on track is what makes for a successful term in office. Your task is to keep all the balls in the air and land some in the success box. Studies have shown that board chairs often feel like a conductor. Sweet music takes all parties involved to play the right notes.

Another task of a good leader is to be apprised of the donors and stakeholders that are involved. Demonstrating strong leadership skills is what gives the donors confidence to give more.

Remember that feelings do matter. Most often, those that serve on your board are also contributing their money to the organization. Their time and skills are also a valuable commodity. Address conflicts head-on and be open to listening closely so that you can make an informed decision that meets the needs of the board members, staff, volunteers, and the organization. Remember that all their feelings matter.

Keep in mind that board members are usually there because they are passionate about what the organization accomplishes. They can be your best ambassadors when their passion aligns with the organization's leadership and goals.

If your organization has an executive director or CEO, you must work closely with them. Make sure that they can meet not only their obligations to the organization but can grow with changes that have been implemented by the board. I can't stress this enough, communication, communication, communication!!! When starting on the board, try to make sure that your one on one meetings are not when the person you are meeting with has a complaint, or you need a favor from them. Please make your first meeting with them positive and open. Take the information you learn from them and about them and use it wisely. If there are pre-existing issues with the person, deal with those issues first.

Another challenge early on for a board chair is to feel overwhelmed by other board members, staff, and volunteers bombarding you with issues and ideas. It is a fairly common experience for many board chairs. You can feel like you are never doing enough and are being hit with a fair amount of negativity. Be sure to practice self-care during your term. Understand that you will not always win, so savor the wins and chalk the misses up to learning. You cannot make everyone happy. When possible, please explain why the unhappy person needs to accept the decision or action that made them unhappy. Again, empathy goes a long way.

Serving as a non-profit board chair/president is often challenging. When you use yours and others' skillsets for the best interest of the organization, on the final day of your term, you can look back with pride at what you have accomplished.

The balls in your court

I have done my best to give you the information and some tools to begin making positive changes to not only your leadership skills but to your personal life. I have repeated essential points in different ways because we all respond differently to what we are being told. Reading these points with different wording may create a positive response I am seeking from you.

Know that while change is always possible, it takes effort and patience.

The key to making improvements in your life is, to be honest with yourself. Ask the opinions of friends and family when possible. While every person has a particular part of one's personality that they tend to focus on, look at the totality of all their comments. The statements that they make that match each other are most likely to be the actual areas you need to put your focus on improving. The areas that they all agree on from a positive aspect are indicative of your current strengths.

Even if you're not able to make some of the changes you would like to, pay attention to others, and learn about their strengths and weaknesses. It will still prove to be invaluable to you having a more positive interaction with them as a leader.

References

Ackerman, Courtney. "Emotional Intelligence and Leadership Effectiveness + 69 Exercises." Positive Psychology Program Website, January 4, 2019.

Bariso, Justin. "How to Increase Your Emotional Intelligence." *Inc.* April 11, 2016. A Short Guide to Start Making Emotions Work for You, Instead of Against You. Web. December 01, 2018.

"What is Emotional Intelligence? Not What You Think," September 29, 2016.

Bradberry, Travis. "9 Things Emotionally Intelligent People Won't Do." *Forbes* March 26, 2014. Emotional Intelligence in Business. Web. December 01, 2018.

Cummins, Denise Ph D. "The Dark Side of Emotional Intelligence." Psychology Today Online, August 15, 2014.

Freedman, Joshua. "How to Improve Emotional Intelligence: 10 Tips for Increasing Self-Awareness." 6seconds Website, 2018.

Golhar, Abhi. "10 Ways to Increase Your Emotional Intelligence" (Inc. this morning newsletter), September 21, 2018.

Grinnell, Renee. "Facial Feedback Hypothesis." *Psych Central* (2016). Web. November 05, 2018. Langley, Sue. "What Emotional Intelligence Test Should I Use?" *Langley Group*. Emotional Intelligence.

August 6, 2012. Web. December 1, 20018.

McCrimmon, Mitch. "Why Emotional Intelligence is not Essential for Leadership." *Ivey Business Journal*

January / February 2009 January 1, 2009. Web. November 18, 2018.

Nayar, Vineet. "Three Differences Between Managers and Leaders." Leadership Transitions. *HarvardBusiness Review* August 2, 2013.

Ryan, Liz. "Forbes." *Management Vs. Leadership: Five Ways They Are Different*. March 27, 2016. Forbes Magazine. Web. November 03, 2018.

Schwartz, Tony. "The Importance of Naming Your Emotions." New York Times, April 3, 2015.

Sporleder, John. "Emotional Intelligence in the Business Workplace." *Comp Communication*. September 13, 2010. Web. November 03, 2018.

Stevenson, Herb. "Leadership Style, Emotional Intelligence, and Organizational Effectiveness." Cleveland Consulting Group, Inc, 2019. Web. April 13, 2019.

Tobak, Steve. "Emotional Intelligence." *Don't Believe the Hype Around Emotional Intelligence*.

September 16, 2014. Entrepreneur Magazine. Web. November 03, 2018.

Tull, Matthew, and PhD. "The Importance of Emotional Awareness in PTSD." *Very well Mind* July 10, 2018. Coping. Web. 5 November 2018.

Whitbourne, Ph D. Susan Krauss. "Why the Emotionally Intelligent May Earn More Money." *Psychology Today* October 3, 2017. New Research Shows Whether or not It Pays to Have a Higher EQ. Web. November 18, 20018.

Whitbourne, Susan Krauss. "The Complete Guide to Understanding Your Emotions." *Psychology Today*

May 19, 2012.

Young, Karen. "19 Practical, Powerful Ways to Build Social-Emotional Intelligence in Kids & Teens." Hey Sigmund Website, 2018.